SRa®

MULTIPLE SKILLS
SERIES: Reading

Third Edition

Richard A. Boning

**SRA
McGraw-Hill**

2

Columbus, Ohio

A Division of The **McGraw·Hill** *Companies*

SRA/McGraw-Hill

A Division of The McGraw·Hill Companies

Send all inquiries to:
SRA/McGraw-Hill
250 Old Wilson Bridge Road
Suite 310
Worthington, Ohio 43085

ISBN 0-02-688423-2

1 2 3 4 5 6 7 8 9 SCG 02 01 00 99 98 97

PURPOSE

The *Multiple Skills Series* is a nonconsumable reading program designed to develop a cluster of key reading skills and to integrate these skills with each other and with the other language arts. *Multiple Skills* is also diagnostic, making it possible for you to identify specific types of reading skills that might be causing difficulty for individual students.

FOR WHOM

The twelve levels of the *Multiple Skills Series* are geared to students who comprehend on the pre-first- through ninth-grade reading levels.

- The Picture Level is for children who have not acquired a basic sight vocabulary.
- The Preparatory 1 Level is for children who have developed a limited basic sight vocabulary.
- The Preparatory 2 Level is for children who have a basic sight vocabulary but are not yet reading on the first-grade level.
- Books A through I are appropriate for students who can read on grade levels one through nine respectively. Because of their high interest level, the books may also be used effectively with students functioning at these levels of competence in other grades.

The **Multiple Skills Series Placement Tests** will help you determine the appropriate level for each student.

PLACEMENT TESTS

The Elementary Placement Test (for grades Pre-1 through 3) and the Midway Placement Tests (for grades 4–9) will help you place each student properly. The tests consist of representative units selected from the series. The test books contain two forms, X and Y. One form may be used for placement and the second as a post-test to measure progress. The tests are easy to administer and score. Blackline Masters are provided for worksheets and student performance profiles.

THE BOOKS

This third edition of the *Multiple Skills Series* maintains the quality and focus that have distinguished this program for over 25 years. The series includes four books at each level, Picture Level through Level I. Each book in the Picture Level through Level B contains 25 units. Each book in Level C through Level I contains 50 units. The units within each book increase in difficulty. The books within a level also increase in difficulty—Level A, Book 2 is slightly more difficult than Level A, Book 1, and so on. This gradual increase in difficulty permits students to advance from one book to the next and from one level to the next without frustration.

Each book contains an **About This Book** page, which explains the skills to the students and shows them how to approach reading the selections and questions. In the lowest levels, you should read About This Book to the children.

The questions that follow each unit are designed to develop specific reading skills. In the lowest levels, you should read the questions to the children.

In Level D, the question pattern in each unit is
1. Title (main idea)
2. Stated detail
3. Stated detail
4. Inference or conclusion
5. Vocabulary

The **Language Activity Pages** (LAP) in each level consist of four parts: Exercising Your Skill, Expanding Your Skill, Exploring Language, and Expressing Yourself. These pages lead the students beyond the book through a broadening spiral of writing, speaking, and other individual and group language activities that apply, extend, and integrate the skills being developed. You may use all, some, or none of the activities in any LAP; however, some LAP activities depend on preceding ones. In the lowest levels, you should read the LAPs to the children.

In Levels C-I, each set of Language Activity Pages focuses on a particular skill developed through the book. Emphasis progresses from the most concrete to the most abstract:

First LAP	Details
Second LAP	Vocabulary
Third LAP	Main ideas
Last LAP	Inferences and conclusions

SESSIONS

The *Multiple Skills Series* is basically an individualized reading program that may be used with small groups or an entire class. Short sessions are the most effective. Use a short session every day or every other day, completing a few units in each session. Time allocated to the Language Activity Pages depends on the abilities of the individual students.

SCORING

Students should record their answers on the reproducible worksheets. The worksheets make scoring easier and provide uniform records of the children's work. Using worksheets also avoids consuming the books.

Because it is important for the students to know how they are progressing, you should score the units as soon as they've been completed. Then you can discuss the questions and activities with the students and encourage them to justify their responses. Many of the LAPs are open-ended and do not lend themselves to an objective score; for this reason, there are no answer keys for these pages.

A careful reader thinks about the writer's words and pays attention to what the story or article is mainly about. A careful reader also "reads between the lines" because a writer does not tell the reader everything. A careful reader tries to figure out the meaning of new words too. As you read the stories and articles in this book, you will practice all of these reading skills.

First you will read a story and choose a good title for it. The title will tell something about the **main idea** of the article or story. To choose a good title, you must know what the story or article is mainly about.

The next two questions will ask you about facts that are stated in the story or article. To answer these questions, read carefully. Pay attention to the **details.**

The fourth question will ask you to figure out **something the writer doesn't tell you directly.** For example, you might read that Dr. Fujihara received an emergency call, drove to Elm Street, and rushed into a house. Even though the writer doesn't tell you directly, you can figure out that Dr. Fujihara knows how to drive and that someone in the house is probably sick. You use the information the author provides plus your own knowledge and experience to figure out what is probably true.

The last question will ask you to tell the meaning of a word in the story or article. You can figure out what the word means by studying its **context**—the other words and sentences in the story. Read the following sentences.

The house was surrounded by trees. They helped keep the house cool in summer. Unfortunately, they also cut out most of the light. A giant *hemlock* just outside Marcia's window made her room dark and gloomy.

Did you figure out that a hemlock is a kind of tree? What clues in the story helped you figure this out?

This book will help you practice your reading skills. As you learn to use all of these skills together, you will become a better reader.

One day a woman in Milford, New Jersey, went to look at her garden. To her surprise, a large turtle was eating her tomatoes. The woman put the turtle in her car and took it to a woods a mile and a half away. Two weeks later she again found the turtle eating her tomatoes. She couldn't be sure if it was the same one, so she put a *dab* of paint on its shell and took it ten miles away.

Turtles are known for their slowness, but four years later the same turtle was in her garden. The woman then made the turtle her pet. She kept it in a pen and fed the turtle its favorite food—tomatoes.

1. The best title is—
   (A) Eating Tomatoes
   (B) How a Turtle Became a Pet
   (C) Coloring Turtle Shells
   (D) Building a Pen for Turtles

2. For the turtle to return from ten miles away took—
   (A) one day   (B) two years
   (C) four weeks   (D) four years

3. The story says that turtles are known for their—
   (A) quickness   (B) horns
   (C) slowness   (D) swimming

4. The woman knew it was the same turtle because of the—
   (A) garden   (B) paint
   (C) apples   (D) pen

5. The word "dab" in line six means—
   (A) paper   (B) spot
   (C) can   (D) picture

In the middle of California's Mojave Desert, silvery pipes gleam in the hot sun. The pipes are part of a special power plant. The plant was first owned by the Luz International Company, and it makes electricity from the rays of the sun.

During the 1970s, many people became interested in solar, or sun, power. Few of them, however, actually did anything about *harnessing* the energy of the sun. Luz was one of the few companies to try. Their hard work has paid off. Though Luz does not own them anymore, the plants still operate. Giant mirrors capture the sun's energy. Each of the plants can make enough electricity to power 100,000 homes. That makes solar power a pretty bright idea.

1. The best title is—
   (A) A Trip to the Desert
   (B) Using Energy from the Sun
   (C) Energy from Many Places
   (D) Silver Pipes in the Sun

2. The solar power plant gets energy from—
   (A) waterfalls
   (B) burning oil
   (C) 100,000 homes
   (D) sunlight

3. Each plant can make power for—
   (A) 16 buildings
   (B) 100,000 homes
   (C) 1,000 homes
   (D) giant mirrors

4. The best place for a solar power plant is—
   (A) in a river valley
   (B) near a big city
   (C) in a sunny area
   (D) near an ocean

5. The word "harnessing" in line six means—
   (A) riding
   (B) making use of
   (C) looking at
   (D) destroying

For thirty years, Dan Stuart ran a clothing store. Each day, he helped customers, ordered new clothing, and made sure everything was in order. In the evening and on weekends, though, Stuart led a completely different life. He was "Globo, the Magic Clown."

Stuart had always loved magic. He learned hundreds of tricks each year. He enjoyed doing shows for friends and local clubs. When he finally was ready to *retire*, he sold the store and gave up his magic shows. Friends and relatives kept asking for Globo, however. Soon he was giving shows all over the area. Now Stuart says, "I'm so busy I can't believe it. I do shows every weekend and even during the week. I think my next big trick will have to be to saw myself in two and make two Globos!"

1. The best title is—
   (A) How to Start a Life in Show Business
   (B) Selling Clothing
   (C) Meet Globo, the Magic Clown
   (D) Stuart's Clothing Store

2. Dan Stuart ran—
   (A) a chemical company   (B) a clothing store
   (C) for mayor   (D) a magic shop

3. Each year, Stuart learned—
   (A) about Globo   (B) new ways to help
   (C) hundreds of tricks   (D) new songs

4. You can tell that Stuart—
   (A) is too old to work   (B) likes being Globo
   (C) misses his store   (D) is paid very well

5. The word "retire" in line seven means—
   (A) sleep   (B) move
   (C) stop working   (D) go home

Would you like to have a pet wolf? Not many people would, of course. However, if scientists are right, your *lovable* pet might very well be the great-great-great grandchild of a wolf.

How did cute, friendly things like dogs come from wolves? According to some scientists, people began training wolves thousands of years ago. The people found that the wolves could help them with many jobs. The wolves also became good pets. In time, say the scientists, the tame wolves were raised with coyotes, wild dogs, and even wild wolves. The result, thousands of years later, was the friendly dog we know today.

1. The best title is—
    (A) How to Train Your Dog to Do Jobs
    (B) From Wolf to Dog in Thousands of Years
    (C) All About Foxes, Coyotes, and Wild Dogs
    (D) Getting to Know Your New Pet Dog

2. Scientists think that, long ago, people—
    (A) bought pets in stores   (B) took home sheep
    (C) trained wild wolves   (D) did not like pets

3. Tame wolves—
    (A) ran wild   (B) helped people
    (C) ate too much   (D) were dangerous

4. You can tell that people long ago—
    (A) wanted wolves to help   (B) knew very little
        them   about wolves
    (C) hated wolves   (D) had lots of pets

5. The word "lovable" in line two means—
    (A) not loved   (B) lovely
    (C) able to be loved   (D) easily moved

Many artists make works of art from clay, iron, or stone. Tony Price, however, was different. His gleaming figures were made from *scrap* metal that came from a bomb laboratory in Los Alamos, New Mexico. That is where a very powerful bomb was first made.

Price learned of the lab's scrap metal in 1965. He made hundreds of works from the pieces of metal he bought from the lab. At first, no one paid attention to Price's unusual art. But then people began to notice his work, and Price sold many pieces. Tony Price's art can still be found in galleries all over the country.

1. The best title is—
    (A) Traveling in New Mexico
    (B) Works of Art from Clay
    (C) Tony Price's Unusual Art
    (D) A Powerful Bomb

2. Tony Price made art from—
    (A) pieces of metal   (B) pieces of wood
    (C) marble   (D) old furniture

3. Price first learned of the metal in—
    (A) a magazine   (B) the past year
    (C) 1965   (D) an art book

4. You can tell that people still—
    (A) don't like his work   (B) like Price's art
    (C) pay no attention   (D) don't know about him

5. The word "scrap" in line two means—
    (A) junk   (B) sharp
    (C) hard   (D) weak

The next time that you hear a baby cry, listen carefully—the baby may be trying to tell you something.

A number of years ago, a doctor in California studied the way babies cry. The doctor believed, as many doctors do today, that each kind of cry means something different. A cry that lasts only a second means the baby is hungry. If the baby is in pain, the cry lasts two or three seconds and is louder. A cry like the *purr* of a kitten means that the baby is happy.

Many doctors and parents think that babies cry because they are trying to tell us how they feel.

1. The best title is—
    (A) What Babies' Cries Mean
    (B) How to Stop Babies from Crying
    (C) Doctors and Parents
    (D) Bringing Up Babies

2. A cry like the purr of a kitten means the baby is—
    (A) in pain   (B) happy
    (C) hungry   (D) playing

3. Many doctors think that babies cry because they—
    (A) are bad   (B) want to tell us something
    (C) like to   (D) want parents to work

4. A baby's cry tells us—
    (A) how it feels   (B) how old it is
    (C) its name   (D) how much it weighs

5. The word "purr" in line seven means—
    (A) fur   (B) paws
    (C) sound   (D) ears

Dictionaries say that "spring fever" is a lazy or restless feeling that people have on the first warm day of spring. Everyone has probably felt it at one time or another. People have talked about it for years.

Recently, scientists have taken a good look at spring fever. What they found is quite surprising.

Where many of us live, the winter months often seem dark and *dreary*. When spring comes in late March, the number of daylight hours grows with each passing day. According to many scientists, all this sunlight sets off chemicals in the brain that change our mood and bring on spring fever.

---

1. The best title is—
    (A) How to Get More Sunshine
    (B) Not Enough Light
    (C) Darkness in the Winter
    (D) Spring Fever

2. Spring fever makes people feel—
    (A) silly   (B) angry
    (C) restless   (D) very smart

3. Scientists think spring fever is caused by—
    (A) birds   (B) sunlight
    (C) air pollution   (D) noise

4. You can tell that chemicals in the brain affect—
    (A) seasons   (B) feelings
    (C) sunlight   (D) looks

5. The word "dreary" in line seven means—
    (A) rainy   (B) snowy
    (C) gloomy   (D) long

Every spring, hundreds of young people from all over the world come to Dallas, Texas. They come to try to win the Dallas Cup. The cup became one of the most important prizes in the sport of *youth* soccer.

The idea for the Dallas Cup was born in 1980. Since then, it has grown bigger and bigger each year. The teams come from everywhere—Canada, England, Thailand, and even the Soviet Union.

The players stay with families all around the Dallas area. Although speaking different languages often can be a problem, most of the kids do quite well. All it takes to make friends is a smile and a soccer ball.

---

1. The best title is—
   (A) Dallas, Texas
   (B) A World of Soccer in One Place
   (C) Learning How to Play Soccer
   (D) A Visit to Dallas

2. The Dallas Cup was born—
   (A) in Canada   (B) a hundred years ago
   (C) in 1980   (D) in 1989

3. Players stay—
   (A) by themselves   (B) far away from Dallas
   (C) with Dallas families   (D) with famous people

4. You can tell that the Dallas Cup has gotten—
   (A) more popular   (B) out of control
   (C) more tiring   (D) less interesting

5. The word "youth" in line three means—
   (A) athletes'   (B) young people's
   (C) not very good   (D) excellent

Mrs. Little saw an ad on television. It was selling trained chickens, but each chicken cost a lot of money. So Mrs. Little decided to train her own. She went to a farm, bought a chicken, and began teaching it.

Mrs. Little knew that chickens love to peck. She *acquired* a toy piano and put food on the keys. The chicken would peck at the piano keys to get the food. Each time the chicken pecked, it would be playing the piano. Soon Mrs. Little had the chicken playing without food on the keys. The chicken knew it would get fed after it finished playing.

Mrs. Little had the only piano-playing chicken in Benld, Illinois—or anywhere!

---

1. The best title is—
   (A) Watching Ads on Television
   (B) Going to a Chicken Farm
   (C) A Chicken That Plays the Piano
   (D) Piano Lessons for Children

2. Mrs. Little bought her chicken—
   (A) from a TV ad   (B) from a friend
   (C) at a store   (D) at a farm

3. The story says that the chicken would peck at the—
   (A) piano keys   (B) kitchen stove
   (C) front door   (D) windows

4. The chicken played the piano because it liked—
   (A) music   (B) food
   (C) studying   (D) Mrs. Little

5. The word "acquired" in line four means—
   (A) listened   (B) lost
   (C) got   (D) sold

Parents who have small children and want to go out, *often* call a babysitter. Did you know that Columbus needed a babysitter when he sailed for America?

Columbus' wife died, leaving him with a five-year-old son named Diego. Columbus had a dream to sail across the ocean to India. So he took his son to a church in Spain. The church people promised to care for Diego while Columbus was away.

Today, if you go to this church in Spain, you can see the room where Diego stayed. You can also see a painting of his famous father, Christopher Columbus.

1. The best title is—
   (A) Life in a Church
   (B) A Famous Painting
   (C) Babysitting for Columbus
   (D) Across the Ocean to India

2. Columbus wanted to sail to—
   (A) Spain   (B) Italy
   (C) India   (D) England

3. When Columbus' wife died, Diego was—
   (A) an old man   (B) five years old
   (C) ten years old   (D) a sailor

4. The church where Diego stayed—
   (A) has been destroyed   (B) has no paintings
   (C) still stands   (D) is in Turkey

5. The word "often" in line one means—
   (A) never   (B) can't
   (C) refuse to   (D) many times

A swan was sleeping on a pond one winter. During the night the weather became very cold. The water turned into ice. The swan couldn't move, and in time it would die.

The swan called, but there was no one to help. Suddenly, a flock of geese came flying by. When they saw the swan stuck in the ice, they landed right by it. Soon they were pecking away at the ice. After a short while, the swan was free. As it *winged* through the air it called a "thank you." Maybe someday the swan would be able to help the geese.

1. The best title is—
   (A) The Color of Swans
   (B) Why Water Turns into Ice
   (C) How Geese Helped a Swan
   (D) Birds That Fly High

2. The geese freed the swan by—
   (A) flying   (B) pecking
   (C) singing   (D) honking

3. To free the swan it took—
   (A) many hours   (B) many years
   (C) a short while   (D) one day

4. When the swan slept, its feet were—
   (A) on the ground   (B) above the water
   (C) kept dry   (D) in the water

5. The word "winged" in line seven means—
   (A) flew   (B) slept
   (C) stayed   (D) lowered

People sometimes do strange things to get attention. Back in the 1920s and 1930s, for example, people used to sit on the top of flagpoles. Some people even made money by sitting on the top of flagpoles. The most famous flagpole sitter was Shipwreck Kelly. His stunts made him famous all over the United States.

One time Kelly sat on the top of a flagpole for thirteen days. Friends sent food and water up the pole to him. One time he even ate while standing on his head on top of the pole. People used to pay to see Kelly perform his stunts. The people said, "Anyone that will sit on a flagpole *deserves* to get paid."

1. The best title is—
   (A) Shipwreck Kelly—Flagpole Sitter
   (B) Stunts Done Long Ago
   (C) Saved from a Shipwreck
   (D) Shipwreck Kelly—Strange Eating Habits

2. The story says that Kelly sat on a flagpole for—
   (A) 3 days   (B) 13 weeks
   (C) 13 days   (D) 6 months

3. As a flagpole sitter, Kelly was—
   (A) unknown   (B) famous
   (C) disliked   (D) always poor

4. The flagpoles people sat on must have been—
   (A) thin   (B) broken
   (C) painted   (D) strong

5. The word "deserves" in line ten means—
   (A) ought never   (B) is stealing
   (C) has a right   (D) is crazy

In Unit 4, you read about how wolves became pets. People everywhere enjoy pets. Pets can guard our homes. They can do all kinds of jobs for us. They can make us laugh with their tricks. But most of all, they can keep us company and be our friends.

What kind of pet would make you happy? Would you like a dog? A cat? Perhaps some fish or a bird?

A. Exercising Your Skill

Think about the kind of pet you might enjoy. What would it be? What would it look like? How would you take care of it? What would you call it? Think about all of these things. Now look at the idea map below, and copy it onto your paper. Fill it in by writing answers under each question.

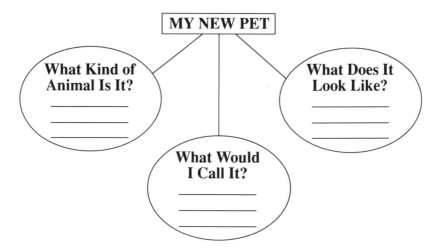

B. Expanding Your Skill

There are many other things to think about if you are going to keep a pet. You must find out how to care for the pet—where it needs to live, what you must feed it, and what else you must do to keep it happy and healthy. You can also think about all the fun you might have with your pet. Add these two questions to your idea map: How Will I Care for It? How Will We Have Fun Together? Then fill in all the answers you can think of.

C. Exploring Language

Imagine that you are writing a letter to a friend about your new pet. What would you say about its size, color, and actions? On your paper, complete this letter. In some blanks, you will use more than one word.

Guess what! I have a new _____. It is _____ and _____. I think having a pet _____ is just great. I like to watch it _____. Sometimes it will _____. If I _____, it will _____.

My book on pet care said I should get _____. Yesterday I went to _____ and bought everything I needed.

Next time you visit, you can see my new friend. By the way, its name is _____.

Your friend,

_____

D. Expressing Yourself

Choose one of these activities.

1. Imagine that you are going away for a week. You have asked your best friend to take care of your pet while you are away. Write out directions for what to do to keep your pet happy and healthy.

2. Suppose you had a very smart pet. What tricks might it do? Make a poster telling people about a show in which your pet will be one of the stars. Put a picture of your pet in the middle. Around the picture, put words telling what your pet will do, why it is fun to see, and when and where the show will be.

3. With a few classmates, write directions for how to teach animals to do some "pet tricks." Share the directions with the class and show how to follow them.

People in Memphis, Tennessee, had a special treat in the Memphis Zoo. For years they had enjoyed Julie, the zoo's hippopotamus. (Hippopotamuses are large animals that live in water.) Then Julie gave birth to a set of 40-pound twins.

People around Memphis made quite a fuss about the two babies. Julie's children were, after all, the first hippo twins ever to be born in the United States. As a result, they had a chance to meet with everyone from city officials to movie stars. Julie, however, was not impressed with all the attention of her well-known guests. In fact, she made sure that no one, not even the zoo's keepers, got close to her young *offspring*. Now, do you think anyone would be willing to argue with a 4,000-pound hippo?

---

1. The best title is—
    (A) Animals in Zoos
    (B) A Guide to the Memphis Zoo
    (C) How to Care for Hippos
    (D) Some Special Babies

2. Julie weighed—
    (A) 40 pounds   (B) 4,000 pounds
    (C) 40,000 pounds   (D) 400 pounds

3. The twins were born—
    (A) in the spring   (B) in the Memphis Zoo
    (C) in the water   (D) in Africa

4. You can tell that Julie's babies became—
    (A) tall   (B) quite famous
    (C) very thin   (D) good swimmers

5. The word "offspring" in line eleven means—
    (A) parents   (B) friends
    (C) children   (D) keepers

By the time that Jim Thunder, a Cree Indian, arrived in New York City, he had run all 2,700 miles from his home in Alberta, Canada.

A few years before, Jim Thunder had a dream about a bundle made from a bear's paw. The bundle had once belonged to a great Cree warrior, Big Bear, and was a symbol of Cree power.

In the dream, Big Bear asked Jim Thunder to find the bundle for the Cree people. Thunder took the dream seriously. After a long search, he finally *located* Big Bear's bundle in New York's Museum of Natural History. Running all the way to New York was his way of calling attention to his belief that Big Bear's bundle should be back home with the Cree people.

---

1. The best title is—
   (A) Big Bear's Dream
   (B) A 2,700-Mile Run
   (C) A History of the Cree People
   (D) Visiting the Museum of Natural History

2. Jim Thunder set out from—
   (A) a museum   (B) Alberta, Canada
   (C) New York City   (D) California

3. The bundle once belonged to—
   (A) Thunder's mother   (B) a museum
   (C) Big Bear   (D) a Mohawk chief

4. You can tell that Jim Thunder—
   (A) dislikes exercise   (B) is a good athlete
   (C) works in New York   (D) is not in good shape

5. The word "located" in line eight means—
   (A) bought   (B) sold
   (C) found   (D) broke

During World War II, the people of Freiberg, Germany, listened to the geese in their park. The geese would cry out with loud squawks whenever enemy airplanes came toward the city. The geese let the people know that enemy bombers were coming, even before the air-raid sirens sounded.

On November 27, 1944, the geese began their noisy *squawks* as they always did before an air raid. Hundreds of people took shelter. A few minutes later, the city of Freiberg was heavily hit by bombs.

After the war, the people of Freiberg built a statue at the entrance of the park. The statue is in honor of the three geese that had been killed in the raid.

---

1. The best title is—
   (A) Geese Help a City
   (B) Building Statues
   (C) Enemy Airplanes
   (D) Raising Geese

2. The people of Freiberg honored the geese by building—
   (A) a tower   (B) a statue
   (C) an airplane   (D) a pond

3. On November 27, 1944, the city of Freiberg was—
   (A) at peace   (B) being built
   (C) bombed   (D) discovered

4. The geese were honored because they—
   (A) gave large eggs   (B) lived in Germany
   (C) warned the people   (D) had beautiful feathers

5. The word "squawks" in line six means—
   (A) loud sounds   (B) tears
   (C) pretty songs   (D) laughs

Kendra's legs felt as if they were going to fall off. It seemed as if she and the other dancers had been practicing for hours.

Kendra knew that all this practice was important. After all, next week was the group's big show. She and the other dancers would perform dances from all over Africa. Hundreds of people would come to watch.

Kendra had started dancing lessons when she was four. She had even come to love the time she spent practicing. Still, all this was very hard work for a seven-year-old girl. Sondra, her teacher, smiled at her. Yes, Kendra thought, we'll all be ready. It will be the best *recital* ever.

1. The best title is—
   (A) Kendra's New Dancing Clothes
   (B) Practice, Practice, Practice
   (C) A Dance That Failed
   (D) A Visit to Africa

2. The group will do dances from—
   (A) North America   (B) Europe
   (C) Africa   (D) Asia

3. Kendra began dance lessons at—
   (A) age seven   (B) age four
   (C) six o'clock   (D) a late age

4. You can tell that Kendra—
   (A) does not like dancing   (B) is not a good dancer
   (C) is a hard worker   (D) enjoys sports

5. The word "recital" in line eleven means—
   (A) practice   (B) march
   (C) dance show   (D) dancing school

Today, thanks to nature lovers, some of the world's *endangered* animals are actually growing in numbers.

Years ago, for example, people who felt that wolves were dangerous killed so many wolves each year that soon they were almost gone. Nature lovers grew worried. They didn't want the wolves to disappear.

Laws were passed to protect the wolves that were left. Wild wolves were captured in Canada and let loose in U.S. forests. Scientists kept track of the wolves to make sure they would live. Soon, wolf packs began to roam the forests of the Midwest.

1. The best title is—
   (A) The Return of the Wolves
   (B) Hunting in the United States
   (C) The Forests of the Midwest
   (D) Life Among the Wolves

2. Years ago, people thought wolves were—
   (A) dangerous
   (B) harmless
   (C) all gone
   (D) better off in Canada

3. Wild wolves were let loose—
   (A) for three years
   (B) in Canada
   (C) in zoos
   (D) in U.S. forests

4. You can tell that many people—
   (A) do not like animals
   (B) have worked to save wolves
   (C) do not like forests
   (D) live in the forest

5. The word "endangered" in line one means—
   (A) long-ago
   (B) wild
   (C) in danger
   (D) worried

Dina waved to her mother. Then, with a push of her flippers, she moved slowly back to the surface. She came up directly under their boat. What a dive!

Dina had grown up in a family of divers. Almost every weekend the family gathered its gear and set off for one diving spot or another. Now it was Dina's turn to learn. She had been nervous at first. The air tanks had seemed heavy and *bulky*. The mask felt tight on her face. Soon, however, she had passed through all her training. This first dive had been wonderful. The sea and its creatures had been all around her. "Hey," she called to her brother up in the boat. "Can this fish come aboard?"

---

1. The best title is—
   (A) The Last Dive
   (B) Dina's First Dive
   (C) Weekend Fishing
   (D) Using Your Air Tank Safely

2. Dina's family went diving—
   (A) once each year   (B) every morning
   (C) on weekends   (D) once each month

3. At first, Dina found the air tanks—
   (A) tight   (B) heavy
   (C) too light   (D) not full

4. You can tell that Dina—
   (A) remained very nervous   (B) did not dive well
   (C) got over being nervous   (D) is afraid of diving

5. The word "bulky" in line seven means—
   (A) too small   (B) too big
   (C) too cold   (D) very fast

Have you ever seen a flamingo? A flamingo is one of those lovely pink birds that you can see standing in a pool of water. What is most unusual, of course, is that flamingos always seem to be *perched* on one leg.

Just why do these large birds spend most of their time on only a single leg? Actually, the answer is quite simple. Because flamingos spend most of their day standing, rather than flying, their legs get very tired. Therefore, the birds simply tuck up one of their legs at a time under their bodies. This keeps their legs rested—and keeps the birds standing.

1. The best title is—
   (A) Lovely Pink Birds
   (B) Why Flamingos Don't Fly
   (C) Why Flamingos Stand on One Leg
   (D) Pink Flamingos

2. Flamingos do not—
   (A) fly much   (B) eat
   (C) stand much   (D) drink water

3. The birds keep one leg—
   (A) over their heads   (B) upside down
   (C) tucked under their bodies (D) in front of the other

4. You can tell that flamingos—
   (A) cannot fly   (B) eat a lot of food
   (C) swim well   (D) live near water

5. The word "perched" in line three means—
   (A) flying   (B) standing
   (C) walking   (D) swimming

Every year, a race unlike any other in the world is held at Loon Mountain, New Hampshire. It is the Loon Mountain Cardboard Box Derby. Hundreds of people come to this small community to take part in it. They race their boxes down a grassy hill.

The rules of the race are simple. Boxes must be made only of cardboard and tape. They also must have at least three sides and a flat bottom. There is only one other rule. At least one person must be in the box when it crosses the finish line.

Since the race began, people have made all kinds of boxes. Recently, one team even built a perfect copy of a real race car completely out of cardboard and tape! As you might *expect*, the car won prizes for the way it looked and for its speed.

1. The best title is—
   (A) Visiting Loon Mountain, New Hampshire
   (B) An Unusual Race
   (C) Winter Sports to Enjoy
   (D) Packing a Cardboard Box

2. The Cardboard Box Derby takes place—
   (A) in Washington, D. C.   (B) at the finish line
   (C) at Loon Mountain   (D) in different places

3. Boxes for the derby must have—
   (A) metal wheels   (B) at least three sides
   (C) small wheels   (D) a crew of three

4. You can tell the boxes are—
   (A) very strong   (B) made of wood
   (C) not all alike   (D) not very big

5. The word "expect" in line eleven means—
   (A) never want   (B) wonder
   (C) think   (D) forget about

You probably have seen many pictures of the black-spotted dogs people call "firehouse" dogs. Did you know that these dogs once had an important job to do?

For hundreds of years, people in Europe used these dogs (which are called Dalmatians) as guards and shepherds and circus performers. Everywhere they went, Dalmatians became known for their speed, their strength, and their *lack* of fear around horses.

In the United States, the people who fight fires quickly found a use for these dogs. The speedy Dalmatians would race ahead of old-time horse-pulled fire trucks, barking to warn people that the trucks were coming. Later, when fire trucks began to use engines instead of horses, the dogs still remained fire-station favorites.

1. The best title is—
   (A) A Special Kind of Dog
   (B) How the Dalmatian Got Its Spots
   (C) Fire Station Rules
   (D) Do You Want to Fight Fires?

2. In Europe, Dalmatians did all of these except—
   (A) run in races   (B) guard things
   (C) work in circuses   (D) take care of sheep

3. In the United States, Dalmatians—
   (A) guarded fire trucks   (B) pulled fire trucks
   (C) ran ahead of fire trucks (D) chased horses

4. You can tell that some dogs—
   (A) pull fire trucks   (B) fear Dalmatians
   (C) cannot bark   (D) fear horses

5. The word "lack" in line seven means—
   (A) too much   (B) not having
   (C) kind   (D) bark

Did you ever wonder how a microwave oven *operates*? Actually, it is quite simple. The oven sends invisible waves of energy, called microwaves, into the food. The waves cause the water inside the food to heat up. As this water heats up, the food cooks from the inside out.

A regular oven, of course, works differently. One reason is that the food cooks from the outside in. First the outside gets hot. Then, as time goes by, more and more of the inside of the food cooks. This is one of the reasons why regular ovens take so much time to cook things. Many people are finding that "inside out" is the right way to go.

---

1. The best title is—
   (A) Using Your Oven
   (B) How to Use Your Microwave Oven
   (C) Inside Out Can Be Better
   (D) Cooking up a Storm

2. In microwave cooking, the first thing that heats up is—
   (A) the outside of food   (B) water in the food
   (C) the middle of food   (D) bones in meat

3. In regular ovens, food cooks—
   (A) too quickly   (B) from the inside out
   (C) from the outside in   (D) only in the middle

4. Microwave ovens may be better than regular ovens when you want food to—
   (A) taste better   (B) cook fast
   (C) look better   (D) be good for you

5. The word "operates" in line one means—
   (A) is put together   (B) works
   (C) breaks   (D) fixes things

Can you picture a fish attacking a submarine? It happened.

A submarine, named the *Alvin,* was near the coast of Georgia when it was attacked by a swordfish. The fish *rammed* into the submarine. It struck so hard that its sword went between the metal plates of the submarine's body. The fish was unable to pull its sword loose.

A flashing light inside the ship showed that the sub was leaking. The captain raised the submarine to the surface. It took two hours for the crew to get the sword from the submarine's body.

That evening the crew enjoyed a swordfish dinner!

---

1. The best title is—
    (A) Building a Submarine
    (B) A Swordfish Attacks a Submarine
    (C) Rising to the Surface
    (D) Cooking a Fish Dinner

2. The submarine was attacked near the coast of—
    (A) Africa   (B) Georgia
    (C) Oregon   (D) Europe

3. A flashing light showed that the submarine was—
    (A) on fire   (B) rising
    (C) leaking   (D) not moving

4. The swordfish that attacked the submarine was—
    (A) finally removed   (B) lost at sea
    (C) bad tasting   (D) very tiny

5. The word "rammed" in line three means—
    (A) missed   (B) hit
    (C) stepped   (D) looked

Every day after school, Rita Sanchez would stop at her grandmother's apartment. Rita and her grandmother both looked forward to these times together. In fact, Rita's grandmother kept saying, "I wish all my other friends had grandchildren to visit them like this."

That gave Rita an idea. She talked with friends about it. Soon, "Kid Visits" was *under way*. Each day, on the way home from school, Kid Visits kids stop and spend time with older people in the neighborhood. The children talk, run errands, or even take the people to the park.

"It's great for everyone," Rita tells people. "People who live alone get to see other people more often. And we get to feel that we have dozens of grandparents!"

---

1. The best title is—
   (A) How to Get Your Errands Done
   (B) A Visit Through the Neighborhood
   (C) Kid Visits
   (D) How Rita Got Rich

2. Every day, Rita would stop and visit—
   (A) her sister   (B) her grandmother
   (C) her brother   (D) her aunt

3. Kid Visits kids do everything but—
   (A) run errands   (B) talk
   (C) clean homes   (D) go to the park

4. You can tell that Kid Visits kids—
   (A) are very unhappy   (B) care about people
   (C) have nothing to do   (D) do well in school

5. The words "under way" in line seven mean—
   (A) beneath the street   (B) not successful
   (C) going on   (D) quiet

In Unit 13, you learned about two baby animals that excited everyone at the Memphis Zoo. Now read some more about zoos. Pay close attention to the underlined words.

Does your community have a zoo? A zoo can be a fantastic place to visit. You can <u>observe</u> many different kinds of animals that you have never seen before except in pictures. Today, many zoos also offer special treats to visitors. Certain sections of the zoo, for example, let people see how animals really live in the <u>wilderness</u>. These sections are set up so that the animals—and the visitors—feel that they are in a real forest, desert, swamp, or other natural area.

Feeding time is a wonderful <u>event</u> that takes place at a zoo. Can you imagine seeing seals jumping and barking to get their fish? And, if that is not exciting enough for you, perhaps you should go during bathing time. What could be more fun than seeing four or five <u>keepers</u> cleaning an elephant with brushes and hoses?

A. Exercising Your Skill

Copy the chart below onto your paper. Then write the clue word or words that helped you figure out the meaning of each underlined word.

WORD	CLUE WORDS
observe	
wilderness	
event	
keepers	

B. Expanding Your Skill

Look up each of the underlined words in a dictionary. Did you find the meaning that you expected? What new things did you learn about the word? Write down the first meaning that the dictionary gives for each word.

C. Exploring Language

Read the words in the box. If you do not know the meaning of some of these words, look them up in a dictionary. Then use all the words to complete the paragraph below. Write the numbers and the words that belong with them on your paper.

lovable	endangered	expect	perch
perform	offspring	exhibits	

Elephants can be great fun to watch, especially if you live in Seattle, Washington. The Seattle Zoo offers one of the best elephant (1) _____ in the world. These huge but (2) _____ animals win everyone's heart. In some parts of the world, elephants are (3) _____ by the large number of hunters, but at the Seattle Zoo, elephants can live and raise their (4) _____ in peace. For the visitors, they are a pleasure to watch. The way they pick up food with their long trunks is much more graceful than you would (5) _____. The elephants can also do some tricks. They will sit, or (6) _____, on large benches, and some will even (7) _____ a short dance.

D. Expressing Yourself

Choose one of these activities.

1. What animal do you think people want to see most in the zoo? Make a poster with a big picture of that animal. Beneath the picture, write three or four sentences about why you think the animal is a favorite.

2. What is the most unusual zoo animal you know of? Use an encyclopedia or other book to find out more about this animal. Then copy these questions on a paper and answer them with the information you found: *What is the animal's name? Where does it come from? What does it look like? How does it behave? What does it eat? Why is it so interesting?*

Are catfish really like cats? Well, on their heads they do have long "feelers" that look a bit like a cat's whiskers. They also make buzzing, croaking sounds that sound a bit like a cat's purr.

Catfish are unusual for many other reasons. Catfish will bite at almost any kind of bait—a worm, a piece of string, or even an old sock. You might think about that the next time you go fishing.

There are many other *odd* catfish. There is an electric catfish that lives in Africa, for example. It can give painful shocks. The strangest of all, however, is a South American catfish that walks across the land to get from one pond or river to another. Now, if that one catches mice, it might really be like a cat!

1. The best title is—
   (A) The Walking Catfish
   (B) Catfish—Unusual Fish
   (C) The African Electric Catfish
   (D) Buying a Catfish

2. Catfish will bite at all of these except—
   (A) a worm   (B) an old sock
   (C) an old tire   (D) a piece of string

3. Catfish make—
   (A) croaking sounds   (B) wonderful pets
   (C) deep dives   (D) good friends

4. You can tell that people probably—
   (A) make catfish soup   (B) race catfish
   (C) fish for catfish   (D) act like catfish

5. The word "odd" in line seven means—
   (A) very thin   (B) common
   (C) unusual   (D) serious

Marty Peters lives in Vermont, and he knows all about maple syrup. Toward the end of each winter, he and his brother Jonah make several gallons of it. All of that syrup comes from trees right on their farm.

They start by drilling holes in their sugar maple trees. With plastic *tubing* they guide the trees' sap, or juice, into plastic bottles. Then they slowly "boil down" the syrup. After several hours, it is dark brown—and delicious. The Peters brothers sell some of their syrup. The rest they keep for their family. As Marty says, "Making maple syrup is hard work. But for pure, homemade syrup, well, it's worth it."

1. The best title is—
   (A) How to Care for Trees
   (B) Marty Peters' Farm
   (C) Life in Vermont
   (D) Making Maple Syrup

2. Marty fills bottles by using—
   (A) drills
   (B) plastic tubing
   (C) giant boilers
   (D) metal cups

3. The maple sap is boiled down for—
   (A) a few minutes
   (B) many days
   (C) several hours
   (D) no reason

4. You can tell that Marty—
   (A) hates maple syrup
   (B) really likes syrup
   (C) does no work at all
   (D) eats syrup from stores

5. The word "tubing" in line six means—
   (A) bathtubs
   (B) flowers
   (C) tubes
   (D) hands

In southern Africa there is a very special snake called the "spitting cobra." This unusual snake is as dangerous as it is beautiful. However, unlike many other dangerous snakes, the spitting cobra usually does not bother to bite its enemies.

When an enemy gets near, a spitting cobra raises up its head. Then it seems to spit right at its enemy's eyes. The cobra's deadly *venom* is squirted through two tiny holes in its fangs, or teeth. If that poison lands in the eyes, it can cause someone to go blind almost immediately. Oddly enough, the poison is completely harmless if it lands on the skin. Even more surprising is the cobra's aim. Spitting cobras have been known to hit an enemy's eyes from as far away as six feet.

1. The best title is—
   (A) Snake Bite
   (B) The King Cobra
   (C) The Strange Spitting Cobra
   (D) How to Take Care of Snake Bites

2. The spitting cobra lives in—
   (A) North America
   (B) Southeast Asia
   (C) southern Africa
   (D) Europe

3. The spitting cobra is different from other snakes because it—
   (A) is very short
   (B) is very long
   (C) has legs
   (D) doesn't bite

4. For safety near spitting cobras you should wear—
   (A) long pants
   (B) heavy boots
   (C) safety goggles
   (D) mittens

5. The word "venom" in line six means—
   (A) water
   (B) poison
   (C) cure
   (D) tooth

Tamara Shamp learned to roller skate before she could walk!

When Tamara was born, the muscles in her legs were not as long as they should be. As she grew and tried to walk, she would *stumble*. Mrs. Shamp thought that if she put roller skates on Tamara's shoes, she would be able to roll where she wanted to go. Also, the skating might stretch her leg muscles and make them longer. Mrs. Shamp was correct. Tamara learned to skate, and soon her legs were well.

Tamara learned to walk and run as well as anyone. Most of the time, however, Tamara said that she would rather be on roller skates.

1. The best title is—
    (A) Special Shoes
    (B) Roller Skating Lessons
    (C) Playing with Other Children
    (D) A Girl Skates Before Walking

2. When Tamara was born, her leg muscles were—
    (A) not thick   (B) not short enough
    (C) not long enough   (D) perfect

3. Mrs. Shamp thought that skates might—
    (A) make Tamara fall   (B) stretch Tamara's muscles
    (C) be bad for Tamara   (D) hurt Tamara

4. Tamara learned to skate when she was—
    (A) very young   (B) a teenager
    (C) twenty years old   (D) fifty years old

5. The word "stumble" in line three means—
    (A) run fast   (B) fall down
    (C) get up   (D) go away

Students in Lake Worth, Texas, go to a school that is different from most other schools in America—it is underground!

There is an air force base near Lake Worth. The jet airplanes that take off and land at the base pass directly over the school. Before the school was moved underground, the pupils couldn't even hear their teachers. The noise was *deafening*!

The main floor of the school is 24 feet under the earth. The school has air conditioning, beautiful classrooms, a cafeteria, and science labs. Best of all, there is no noise from the airplanes.

1. The best title is—
   (A) An Air Force Base in Texas
   (B) Beautiful Classrooms
   (C) Going to School Underground
   (D) A Noisy School

2. The school in the story is—
   (A) in California   (B) very old
   (C) 24 miles from town   (D) 24 feet underground

3. The story says that the school has—
   (A) a gym   (B) science labs
   (C) offices   (D) a flagpole

4. The school in the story probably does *not* have any—
   (A) bathrooms   (B) walls
   (C) windows   (D) doors

5. The word "deafening" in line six means—
   (A) interesting   (B) not loud
   (C) very loud   (D) funny

The street lamps are shaped like chocolate candy kisses. The streets have names like East Chocolate Avenue. You are in Chocolate Town, U.S.A. Its real name is Hershey, Pennsylvania.

In 1905, a man named Milton Hershey opened a chocolate factory in a cornfield. Today there are thousands of people living in the town. Visitors are amazed at the huge *vats* that hold ten thousand pounds of chocolate each. It takes milk from fifty thousand cows every day to help make the candy. There are barns holding 90 million pounds of cacao beans. Chocolate is made from cacao beans.

If you are ever near Hershey, Pennsylvania, stop at the world's largest chocolate factory. There are free samples, too!

1. The best title is—
   (A) Free Samples
   (B) Chocolate Town, U.S.A.
   (C) Chocolate Cake
   (D) Cacao Beans and Milk

2. Every day the factory uses the milk from—
   (A) 7,000 cows   (B) 1,905 cows
   (C) 50,000 cows   (D) 90 million cows

3. To make chocolate, you need milk and—
   (A) cacao beans   (B) samples
   (C) corn   (D) barns

4. From the size of the factory, you can tell that people like—
   (A) milk   (B) cacao beans
   (C) chocolate   (D) visitors

5. The word "vats" in line six means—
   (A) people   (B) beans
   (C) cups   (D) tanks

Scientists have found out something that the Inuit have known for centuries—igloos are good homes.

In 1969, a group of scientists went to the North Pole to study the weather. They took an Inuit named Levi. The scientists had brought fiberglass houses and double-walled tents to live and *store* their equipment in. It didn't take long for them to discover that Levi's igloo of snow was better. The igloo was airtight and kept the heat better. The equipment was safer inside the igloo, and the scientists were more comfortable. Levi built a number of igloos and everyone was happy.

1. The best title is—
   (A) Living in Tents
   (B) The Igloo—A Good Home
   (C) Studying the Weather
   (D) Storing Equipment at the North Pole

2. The story says that igloos are made of—
   (A) stone   (B) snow
   (C) cloth   (D) wood

3. Levi built—
   (A) a fort   (B) a double-walled tent
   (C) new equipment   (D) a number of igloos

4. The story suggests that scientists at the North Pole—
   (A) cooked outside   (B) learned to fish
   (C) found firewood   (D) used igloos

5. The word "store" in line five means—
   (A) sell   (B) break
   (C) keep   (D) lose

Drivers around San Francisco have a hard time keeping their eyes on the road. This is because there are so many interesting things to see!

People have used the driftwood that washes up on the shore to make huge statues. Some of the statues are 18 feet high. Since 1965, these giant objects have been placed along the sides of roads. There have been a headless horse rider, a huge hand, an airplane, and even Snoopy and the Red Baron!

The drivers around San Francisco *wonder* what they will see next. The police hope that it is not an accident because a driver was not watching the road.

---

1. The best title is—
   (A) Fun at the Shore
   (B) Horses and Airplanes
   (C) Statues Around San Francisco
   (D) Careful Drivers

2. One statue in the story was of—
   (A) an elephant   (B) a huge ear
   (C) a hand   (D) an apple

3. The huge statues are made of—
   (A) metal   (B) glass
   (C) driftwood   (D) plastic

4. The story suggests that the statues—
   (A) are popular   (B) are growing smaller
   (C) are all broken   (D) help the police

5. The word "wonder" in line eight means—
   (A) write down   (B) drive away from
   (C) think about   (D) forget

A wishing well is usually a small pool or well with a little water in it. People throw coins in the wishing well and make a wish. They hope that throwing coins in the well will make their wish come true.

One wishing well is different from most because it is a big pool in the Luray Caverns in Virginia. Thousands of visitors come to this huge wishing well, make a wish, and then throw in a coin or two. The pool is so big, and so many visitors *fling* coins into it, that the bottom is almost always covered with money—sometimes thousands of dollars! The money is later collected and given to organizations of people who are looking for new medicines and new cures for diseases.

---

1. The best title is—
   (A) A Huge Wishing Well
   (B) How to Save Money
   (C) Visiting Virginia
   (D) Fishing in a Wishing Well

2. The Luray Caverns are in—
   (A) New Jersey   (B) Nevada
   (C) Virginia   (D) Ohio

3. People who throw money in a wishing well usually—
   (A) become rich   (B) get wet
   (C) have no friends   (D) make a wish

4. The story suggests that the Luray Caverns are—
   (A) dangerous   (B) popular
   (C) very small   (D) brand new

5. The word "fling" in line seven means—
   (A) buy   (B) make
   (C) throw   (D) find

How could a little canary save someone's life? It happened to an eighty-year-old lady in Tennessee.

The lady lived alone with a canary as a pet. Her niece was reading at her own home when she heard a noise at her window. It kept getting louder and louder. Finally she went to the window. There was the little canary *fluttering* its wings against the window.

Feeling there was something wrong, the niece drove to her aunt's house. The lady had struck her head on a table and was bleeding badly. The niece called a doctor and the lady was saved—thanks to her pet canary.

---

1. The best title is—
   (A) Calling a Doctor
   (B) Raising Canaries
   (C) How Accidents Can Happen
   (D) A Canary Saves a Life

2. When the canary was at the window, the niece was—
   (A) sewing   (B) eating
   (C) reading   (D) washing

3. The lady had struck her head on a—
   (A) bookcase   (B) table
   (C) door   (D) lamp

4. The canary saved the lady's life by giving—
   (A) blood   (B) a present
   (C) a warning   (D) first aid

5. The word "fluttering" in line six means—
   (A) tasting   (B) moving
   (C) sleeping   (D) singing

There is only one precious jewel not mined from the earth. This jewel is the pearl. Pearls are used mostly for necklaces and rings. They are expensive because it is difficult to get them.

Pearls are found in oysters. Oysters are small sea animals that live in shells. When a grain of sand gets into the shell, the oyster puts a smooth coating on it. The coating protects the oyster from the sand. This becomes a pearl. As the oyster puts on more layers, the pearl "grows." Divers go deep into the ocean to *gather* oysters. Only one oyster in thousands contains a pearl. You can understand why pearls are valuable.

---

1. The best title is—
    (A) Grains of Sand
    (B) The Valuable Pearl
    (C) Brave Divers
    (D) Eating Oysters

2. Most pearls are—
    (A) cheap   (B) yellow
    (C) expensive   (D) square

3. Pearls are used for—
    (A) cooking   (B) fishing
    (C) necklaces   (D) games

4. Pearls are formed in animals that live in the—
    (A) ground   (B) water
    (C) air   (D) jungle

5. The word "gather" in line eight means—
    (A) store   (B) make
    (C) wear   (D) collect

Skip Wilson wanted to build a small house, but he didn't have much money. Then he had an idea. His brother worked at a dump where people often threw away things that were still good. Skip thought he would go to the dump every day and get all the materials he could to build his house.

Skip's idea worked out very well. He built a one-room house that had a shingled roof, four windows, a door, rugs for the floor, and a wood-burning stove. The only thing Skip had to buy was nails—and they only cost two dollars and thirty cents.

Skip's house may not have been a *palace*, but it was his own.

---

1. The best title is—
   (A) The High Cost of Building
   (B) An Old Stove
   (C) A Rich Man
   (D) Building a House Cheaply

2. Skip Wilson got most of the materials from—
   (A) a large store   (B) a small store
   (C) a dump   (D) friends

3. Skip's house—
   (A) is very large   (B) is painted green
   (C) has no windows   (D) has one room

4. To build the whole house cost Skip—
   (A) nothing   (B) $2.30
   (C) $10.00   (D) $50.00

5. The word "palace" in line ten means—
   (A) small house   (B) very fine house
   (C) roof   (D) game

Tracy Grant's arms were tired. Could she go any farther? Quickly, Grant told herself that this was no time to quit. Only half a mile remained to the finish line. She just had to finish!

The long race, called a marathon, had begun hours earlier. At the sound of the starter's gun, over a hundred people had started out. Now everyone was stretched out along the twenty-six miles of the course. However, it looked as if almost all of them would finish.

Grant pushed harder. Looking back, she could tell she was getting farther and farther ahead. Her first *victory* in a wheelchair marathon was almost hers!

1. The best title is—
   (A) Tracy Grant
   (B) Tracy Grant's Race
   (C) A Marathon
   (D) Exercise for Health

2. The marathon had begun—
   (A) hours earlier   (B) at six o'clock
   (C) late   (D) toward noon

3. Tracy Grant felt—
   (A) lonely   (B) tired
   (C) rested   (D) sad

4. You can tell that Tracy Grant is—
   (A) a quitter   (B) very selfish
   (C) very determined   (D) quite smart

5. The word "victory" in line nine means—
   (A) turn   (B) loss
   (C) win   (D) start

Have you ever seen a pine tree at the top of a building that was being put up? If so, have you ever wondered why?

Years ago, people in Europe started putting trees on the tops of new houses. Placing a tree there was a way for the builders to wish good *fortune* to the people who would be living in the new house.

As time went on, placing a tree on a building took on other meanings as well. Many builders place trees on the top beams of tall city buildings before they put up the walls. This is their way of saying, "This is as tall as this building will get." Other builders say they put trees on finished buildings to show that no one was seriously hurt while the building was going up.

---

1. The best title is—
   (A) Growing Trees on Housetops
   (B) Trees on Tops of Buildings
   (C) Indoor Gardening in the City
   (D) How to Plant Trees

2. Putting trees on tops of new houses started in—
   (A) America   (B) Africa
   (C) Europe   (D) Asia

3. On tall city buildings, trees sometimes show—
   (A) where a building is   (B) the first floor
   (C) the doorways   (D) how tall a building is

4. You can tell that putting trees on buildings is—
   (A) for decoration   (B) a new idea
   (C) for birds to nest   (D) an old custom

5. The word "fortune" in line five means—
   (A) fun   (B) luck
   (C) food   (D) help

You have read a lot about some unusual animals. Now read about an unusual person who is helping to save the world's animals.

Gerald Durrell has always loved animals. When he was growing up, his brother and sister never really got used to his magpies, scorpions, and other strange pets.

As he grew older, Durrell realized that many of the world's animals were in danger of dying out. Some were disappearing because of hunters. Others were dying because their forest homes were being turned into farms.

Gerald Durrell decided to build a zoo especially for endangered animals. Today, Durrell's zoo has some of the rarest animals in the world. There are mountain gorillas from Africa, snow leopards from India, and parrots from the Caribbean. These animals all get special attention. They are also part of an unusual school. People from all over the world go to this school to learn about the animals. They also learn how to prevent the animals in their own countries from dying off.

A. Exercising Your Skill

Think about Durrell and his zoo. Then read these lists. On your paper, write a heading that tells what each list is about.

DURRELL'S ZOO

(Heading)	_(Heading)_
has rare animals	mountain gorillas
cares for animals	snow leopards
teaches others about animals	parrots

B. Expanding Your Skill

Write a paragraph that begins with one of these two sentences: _I agree that saving animals is important,_ or _I do not agree that saving animals is important._ After your opening sentence, write your reasons.

C. Exploring Language

Read each paragraph. On your paper, write a title that gives the main idea of the paragraph.

1. It was not easy for Durrell to start his zoo. He needed a lot of help. He also needed a lot of money. He had to pay to bring in animals. He also had to pay keepers and helpers. At first there seemed to be no way to raise the money. Then Durrell's brother suggested that people would love to read about animals. Since then, Gerald Durrell has written dozens of books to help pay the costs of his special zoo.

2. Baby animals are an important part of Durrell's zoo. Since most of the animals in the zoo have been disappearing from the earth, the babies that are born in the zoo help build up the number of these animals. Then, when it is safe, the animals can be returned to their own homelands. Some of the babies are also given to other zoos.

D. Expressing Yourself

Choose one of these activities.

1. Write a newspaper article about a kind of animal that is dying out. Tell what the animal is, what it is like, and why it is in danger of disappearing. You can find information by looking under *Endangered species* in an encyclopedia or index or by asking a librarian for help.

2. Write a story about a boy or girl who rescues an animal from danger. Will the animal be a wild animal, a farm animal, or a pet? What will the danger be—a fire, a storm, a hunter, another animal? How will the boy or girl rescue the animal, and why? As you think about these ideas, jot down some notes. Then write your story. Try to make it exciting!

Mikile lives far to the north, in Greenland. He is one of the Inuit people. They live much as Eskimos have for hundreds of years. Today, though, is an important one for Mikile. He is now old enough to be a real Inuit hunter.

With the other hunters, Mikile is in a small boat. They paddle slowly in order to sneak up on a herd of six narwhals. A narwhal is a three-thousand-pound whale with a single long horn in its *forehead*. Coming within a few feet of one of the whales, Mikile throws his harpoon. The other hunters quickly paddle over to help. Still fighting against the strong whale, Mikile is pleased. There will be food for the family during the long Greenland night.

1. The best title is—
   (A) Life Among the Inuit
   (B) Narwhals
   (C) Mikile's Hunt
   (D) Traveling in Greenland

2. Narwhals—
   (A) are small and fast
   (B) weigh 3,000 pounds
   (C) are boats
   (D) are harpoons

3. The hunters' weapons are—
   (A) harpoons
   (B) knives
   (C) bows and arrows
   (D) clubs

4. You can tell that for the Inuit—
   (A) whales are pets
   (B) fighting is fun
   (C) food is scarce
   (D) life is easy

5. The word "forehead" in line seven means—
   (A) tail
   (B) flipper
   (C) part above the eyes
   (D) lower part of the back

Thousands of years ago, a clever person strapped a board to each foot and skied off down a snowy mountain. These days, people use just one board—a snowboard.

Snowboarding is one of the fastest-growing winter sports. Many ski resorts now offer classes to beginners of all ages. Some even provide special areas where more experienced snowboarders can practice jumps and spins. *Seasoned* skiers are switching to snowboarding, or "riding," when they take to the slopes.

The next time you go to a ski resort, you may want to leave your skis at home. But don't forget to pack your parka and your sunscreen!

1. The best title is—
   (A) Hit the Slopes
   (B) The Last Resort
   (C) No Skis Allowed
   (D) A Fast-Growing Winter Sport

2. A good place to learn snowboarding is—
   (A) a slope   (B) in the street
   (C) a ski resort   (D) a skating rink

3. Snowboarding is also called—
   (A) poling   (B) riding
   (C) switching   (D) gliding

4. The story suggests that today more people are learning—
   (A) skiing   (B) jumping
   (C) sledding   (D) snowboarding

5. The word "seasoned" in line seven means—
   (A) spicy   (B) experienced
   (C) falling   (D) grabby

Elizabeth Billington sang in an opera in Naples, Italy. She was a singer from England who was famous for her strong voice. That was on May 30, 1794.

Two weeks later, Mount Vesuvius, a huge volcano, erupted. People began to talk. Some people said that Billington had caused the volcano to erupt by singing so loudly. They said that her strong voice had shaken the mountain.

This, of course, was *nonsense*. No voice could be loud enough to shake a mountain. But some people believed it. Soon they became so angry that Billington had to leave Naples. She was probably the only singer ever blamed for causing a volcano to erupt.

1. The best title is—
   (A) Elizabeth Billington's Soft Voice
   (B) Elizabeth Billington Gets Blamed
   (C) A Visitor to Naples, Italy
   (D) A Peaceful Volcano

2. Elizabeth Billington was a singer from—
   (A) England   (B) Spain
   (C) China   (D) America

3. Billington was famous for—
   (A) being friendly   (B) her soft voice
   (C) her strong voice   (D) escaping

4. When Billington left Naples, she was probably—
   (A) cold   (B) ready to retire
   (C) very old   (D) afraid

5. The word "nonsense" in line eight means—
   (A) a good idea   (B) a foolish idea
   (C) true   (D) very possible

Just about everyone believes that cats land on their feet when they fall. However, does this really happen?

Surprisingly, cats actually do land on their feet most of the time. Cats have an unusual *reflex* that helps them turn themselves right side up. Just as people blink their eyes or breathe without ever thinking about it, cats almost always can keep their feet pointed toward the ground. That is why they twist around in the air and come down on the ground feet first. As you might think, though, as cats get heavier or older, they tend to lose their ability to turn over in the air.

1. The best title is—
   (A) Caring for Your Cat
   (B) Why Cats Land Right Side Up
   (C) How to Keep Your Cat Trim
   (D) Training Your Cat to Turn Over

2. Cats usually do land—
   (A) on their backs   (B) on their feet
   (C) sideways   (D) and hurt themselves

3. Cats lose their strange gift when they get—
   (A) too skinny   (B) too high up
   (C) heavier or older   (D) dizzy

4. This special ability of cats probably helps them—
   (A) surprise people   (B) avoid getting fat
   (C) find food   (D) avoid getting hurt

5. The word "reflex" in line four means—
   (A) meal   (B) something happy
   (C) something done without (D) muscle
       thinking

More than 2,000 years ago, Emperor Shih Huang Ti of the Ch'in dynasty ruled in China. In fact, it was his dynasty that gave China its name. When the emperor died, he was buried in a huge tomb. Stories about a magnificent army standing guard over the tomb were passed down from generation to generation. But no one knew whether the stories were really true.

One day, workers digging a well in the countryside *unearthed* a life-sized figure of a soldier. It was made out of pottery called "terra cotta." The legendary army had been found! Six thousand warriors, chariot drivers, and horses were arranged in rows around Shih Huang Ti's tomb. They had been keeping watch over their ruler for hundreds of years.

1. The best title is—
   (A) Model Soldiers
   (B) The Emperor's Army
   (C) The Well Diggers
   (D) Chinese Pottery

2. Shih Huang Ti ruled China more than—
   (A) 100 years ago   (B) 20 years ago
   (C) 2,000 years ago   (D) 6,000 years ago

3. Terra cotta is a type of—
   (A) glass   (B) wood
   (C) stone   (D) pottery

4. You can tell that Shih Huang Ti was—
   (A) powerful   (B) brave
   (C) hated   (D) old

5. The word "unearthed" in line seven means—
   (A) caught   (B) struck
   (C) buried   (D) dug up

At one time, Kemp's ridley sea turtles were rapidly approaching extinction. Today, thanks to the National Park Service, their numbers may slowly be increasing.

The program to save the sea turtles has spanned nearly 20 years. In 1978, eggs were collected from the turtles' small nesting site in Mexico and *transported* to Padre Island, off the Texas coast. By 1988, more than 22,000 eggs had been moved. When the eggs hatched, the baby turtles were tagged before they swam away.

It can be 10–15 years before a female turtle returns to where she was born and lays her eggs. Finally, in July 1996, the first 27 Kemp's ridley sea turtle eggs laid on Padre Island hatched. Park Service workers have had to wait a long time to find out whether their project was a success.

---

1. The best title is—
   (A) An Island Near Texas
   (B) The National Park Service
   (C) Saving the Kemp's Ridley Sea Turtle
   (D) How Hatchlings are Tagged

2. The Park Service moved eggs from Mexico to—
   (A) California   (B) Hawaii
   (C) Texas   (D) Baja

3. The program to save the sea turtles has spanned—
   (A) 10–15 years   (B) since 1988
   (C) since July   (D) nearly 20 years

4. So far, only a small number of Padre Island turtles—
   (A) can swim   (B) eat shrimp
   (C) have returned   (D) need shelter

5. The word "transported" in line six means—
   (A) packed   (B) captured
   (C) replaced   (D) moved

The next time you bite into a hot dog, you might think about how it got its name. Three hundred years ago, people in Germany were eating long, thin tubes of meat called "dachshund sausages." The sausages had this name because they looked like the famous dachshund dogs.

By the 1860s, the sausages were being sold from carts on the streets of New York. By the 1870s, there were *stands* for selling sausages at New York's Coney Island.

Then, in the early 1900s, a person selling dachshund sausages at baseball games started yelling, "Get your red hot dachshund sausages." One of the people at the game drew a cartoon of a barking dachshund sausage lying inside its warm bun. Since then, these sausages have been called "hot dogs" all around the world.

1. The best title is—
   (A) The History of Dachshunds
   (B) How to Cook a Hot Dog
   (C) Baseball Treats
   (D) How the Hot Dog Got Its Name

2. Dachshund sausages first came from—
   (A) the United States   (B) Germany
   (C) France   (D) Mexico

3. A picture of a barking sausage was made by—
   (A) a baseball player   (B) a person at the game
   (C) a person selling hot dogs (D) a cook

4. You can tell that hot dogs are—
   (A) now served cold   (B) no longer popular
   (C) often sold outdoors   (D) made for dogs

5. The word "stands" in line seven means—
   (A) boats   (B) large buildings
   (C) long lines   (D) booths

Bzzzz...bzzzzz.... How do flies make that buzzing noise anyway? Do they have something hidden somewhere that makes the noise?

First of all, flies buzz only when they are flying. That is because the noise you hear is the sound of flies' wings. Those wings move very quickly—almost two hundred times each second. In fact, they move so fast that they make a buzzing sound. Mosquitoes also make a buzzing sound when they fly. A mosquito's buzz, however, is not nearly as loud as a fly's.

The *champion* buzz maker, of course, is that very noisy insect called the bumblebee. In fact, the word *bumble* comes to us from an old word that means "humming." Isn't that what the flapping of a bee's wings sounds like?

---

1. The best title is—
   (A) Buzzing Bugs
   (B) Getting Rid of Insects
   (C) Studying Insects
   (D) Mosquitoes and Other Bugs

2. A fly's moving wings make—
   (A) it go slowly   (B) no noise at all
   (C) its buzzing sound   (D) the fly tired

3. A fly's wings move—
   (A) twice a minute   (B) 20 times a second
   (C) 2,000 times a minute (D) 200 times a second

4. You can tell that a bumblebee's buzz is—
   (A) softer than a fly's   (B) never heard
   (C) louder than a mosquito's (D) very slow

5. The word "champion" in line nine means—
   (A) greatest   (B) fastest
   (C) heaviest   (D) oldest

City streets are usually patrolled by police officers on foot, in cars, or on motorcycles. In some places, police get around either on horseback or on bicycles. But what about keeping the peace on skates?

Police officers in Bartlett, Illinois, are trying out a skate patrol. The public response is *positive,* and the officers like it too. Roller-blading through town gives officers a better opportunity to meet and talk with people on the street. They are able to build trust and to promote safety, especially with children.

Don't be surprised if you see police officers on skates cruising the sidewalks of your town sometime soon. They may even join you for a pick-up game of roller hockey!

---

1. The best title is—
   (A) Safety in Bartlett
   (B) The Skate Patrol
   (C) Hockey with Police
   (D) Trusting Children

2. Officers on skates are able to—
   (A) go fast   (B) drive cars
   (C) talk with people   (D) chase criminals

3. Some police officers patrol city streets—
   (A) in dune buggies   (B) on skateboards
   (C) on camels   (D) on bicycles

4. The story suggests that officers on skates may become—
   (A) too dangerous   (B) teachers
   (C) less common   (D) more common

5. The word "positive" in line five means—
   (A) poor   (B) angry
   (C) good   (D) sure

The Washington Monument, in Washington, D.C., is a thrilling sight. Every month thousands of visitors *gaze* at the marble tower that is 555 feet tall. It always looks so bright and clean! Not many people know the work it takes to keep it looking good. Recently, seven months were needed to clean and repair it.

The marble was cracked. Workers on platforms patched the cracks. The monument was next given a complete cleaning. Finally it was painted.

The next time you see a picture of the Washington Monument, think of all the work it takes to keep it looking beautiful.

---

1. The best title is—
   (A) Climbing the Washington Monument
   (B) Keeping the Washington Monument Beautiful
   (C) Scientists Help
   (D) A Good Paint

2. The Washington Monument is—
   (A) 555 feet tall   (B) in Texas
   (C) in Baltimore   (D) perfect

3. The Washington Monument is made of—
   (A) wood   (B) steel
   (C) marble   (D) glass

4. Before the Washington Monument was cleaned it was—
   (A) moved   (B) repaired
   (C) closed   (D) perfect

5. The word "gaze" in line two means—
   (A) run   (B) sleep
   (C) work   (D) look

Have you ever watched a chicken run? Did you notice how it jerks its head? Scientists now know why the chicken does this.

Scientists took slow-motion pictures of chickens running. They studied the pictures very carefully. They found out that the chicken's head does not move back and forth. The head only jerks forward—then the body catches up. When the scientists covered the chicken's eyes, the head no longer jerked at all.

The scientists had found out that the chicken only *thrusts* its head forward to see better. Wouldn't it be funny if most chickens needed glasses?

---

1. The best title is—
   (A) Laying Eggs for People to Eat
   (B) The Work of a Scientist
   (C) Why Chickens Move Their Heads
   (D) Chickens on TV

2. When chickens run, they move their heads—
   (A) forward   (B) backward
   (C) sideways   (D) in all directions

3. The people who studied chickens running were—
   (A) cooks   (B) scientists
   (C) teachers   (D) butchers

4. Slow-motion pictures were taken to—
   (A) ask a question   (B) answer a question
   (C) show on TV   (D) write a book

5. The word "thrusts" in line eight means—
   (A) eats   (B) moves
   (C) sleeps   (D) flies

The helicopter is an unusual and useful machine. It can fly straight up in the air and stay in the same place. People wished for such a machine for many years before it was finally invented.

Toy helicopters appeared in France back in the 1700s. A few years later, an English scientist, Sir George Cayley, tried to use steam engines to run larger helicopters. For more than a hundred years, people tried to make helicopters big enough for people to fly in. By 1910, Igor Sikorsky finally showed the world two such helicopters. These machines flew, but they did little more than fly straight up and down. It took Sikorsky until 1940 to make a real, *practical* helicopter.

1. The best title is—
    (A) The Life of Igor Sikorsky
    (B) The History of Helicopters
    (C) The First Flight
    (D) Flying Through the Air

2. Toy helicopters first appeared in—
    (A) Russia　　　　　　　　(B) England
    (C) France　　　　　　　　(D) New York

3. Cayley tried to run helicopters by using—
    (A) sun power　　　　　　(B) steam engines
    (C) electric power　　　　(D) car engines

4. You can tell that Cayley's helicopters—
    (A) flew high　　　　　　(B) were toys
    (C) held people　　　　　(D) weren't very useful

5. The word "practical" in line ten means—
    (A) toy　　　　　　　　　(B) useful
    (C) never used　　　　　　(D) powerful

"Don't eat junk food!" is a cry people hear almost every day. Just what, exactly, is wrong with junk food?

One of the biggest problems with junk food is fat. Fat in food does help give you energy, and it also gives your body important chemicals. Too much fat, though, can mean big trouble. High-fat foods can make your body store up too much cholesterol. Cholesterol can stop your blood from flowing properly. The result can be heart disease and other health problems.

What do fat and cholesterol have to do with junk food? Well, most health experts say that people should eat no more than 67 grams (2 ounces) of fat each day. But a double cheeseburger with sauce has 61 grams of fat all by itself! Even a regular fast-food hamburger has almost 34 grams of fat. It's easy to see why doctors are worried about people who eat foods like these many times a week.

A. Exercising Your Skill

As you read the paragraphs above, you probably learned some facts. Now, read the sentences below. Which ones tell ideas that you could get by "reading between the lines" of the story? Write those sentences on your paper.

- Too much cholesterol is not good for your body.
- Nobody likes to eat junk food.
- Some fast-food meals have a whole day's supply of fat.
- It's important to eat food each day that has some fat.

B. Expanding Your Skill

Write this sentence on your paper: *People should set a limit to how much high-fat food they eat.* Beneath the sentence, write the facts from the paragraph that show why this statement is true.

C. Exploring Language

Read these paragraphs and add the missing words. Use what you have already learned about junk food to decide what words will make sense in the blanks. Write the finished paragraph on your paper.

Hamburgers are sometimes called _____ food because they contain a lot of fat. This kind of fat also shows up in other foods. Most fast-food _____ serve food that has been fried in oil made from melted beef fat. The oil is used for frying everything from hamburgers to _____ .

Eating foods with too much salt can also be _____ for you. Many _____ say that adults should have only 1,100 to 3,330 milligrams of salt each day. A large fast-food hamburger has over 1,000 _____ of salt. Add salty French fries to that and you have more than a whole day's _____ of salt—all in a single lunch or snack.

D. Expressing Yourself

Choose one of these activities.

1. What do you think you could say to make people eat less junk food? Write an advertisement that would make people want to eat more healthful foods.

2. Is there any kind of healthful food you can make for yourself, such as salad or soup? Write a recipe for this food. First, list all the ingredients. Then explain, step by step, how you prepare the food. Be sure to explain each step very clearly, and list the steps in their correct order. Now go back and read what you wrote. Is someone who follows your recipe sure to get perfect results? Then, if possible, make your recipe and bring it to class for a "tasting party."